THE CARTOGRAPHER SLEEPS

For Anne
with love & best wishes

THE CARTOGRAPHER SLEEPS

BARBARA DANIELS

Barbara Daniels

Shoestring Press

Typeset and printed by Q3 Print Project Management Ltd,
Loughborough, Leics
(01509) 213456

Published by Shoestring Press
19 Devonshire Avenue, Beeston, Nottingham, NG9 1BS
(0115) 925 1827
www.shoestringpress.co.uk

First published 2005
© Copyright: Barbara Daniels
The moral right of the author has been asserted.
ISBN: 1 904886 14 0

Shoestring Press gratefully acknowledges financial assistance from
Arts Council England

CONTENTS

I acknowledge my debt to the editors of the following magazines in which my poems have appeared, with thanks for all the hard work that goes into their task: Borderlines, Candelabrum, Envoi, Equinox, The Interpreter's House, Iota, Links, Manifold, Poetry Nottingham International, Quattrocento, Orbis, Reach and its successor bluechrome Reach.

I am grateful also to the organisers and judges of these competitions who have given their time to the recognition of my work often including it in an anthology or publishing it on the internet: Barnet, The Black Horse, Classic Turkish Van Cats, Diss (Thetford, Wymondham and District), Friends of St. Michael's Discoed, Hastings, Ilkley, Kent and Sussex, Kick Start Poets, Northampton Literature Group, Nottingham Poets, Pitshanger Poets, Poetry on the Lake, Redcar Poets, Roundyhouse, Salopian, Scottish International, Speakeasy and Writers' Bureau.

AFTER THE PARTY

Yesterday the world was double and enveloped in a mist
Like the fog of a pea-souper in November,
And whom I'd met and what I'd said and whom I'd hugged and
    kissed
Were lost forever. I could not remember
Arriving home, crawling upstairs or falling into bed,
(The aftermath is time for second-guessing)
And, because of mini-armies waging war inside my head
I spent a doleful morning convalescing.

The afternoon was better: I had tea and buttered toast
And thought of you (my faculties were clearing):
Handsome, lean, a perfect gentleman, always the thoughtful host
But with little human touches – so endearing!
By evening I was wretched: what must you have made of me
Lurching round your room unsteadily, a danger
To life and limb and peace of mind, a cannon loose at sea,
Telling not-so-funny jokes to any stranger?

This morning is White Monday: everything is crystal bright
Except for me – I'm gloomy with repentance.
I'll email you or perhaps text or maybe even write:
Please don't judge me with a distant prison sentence.
I'll be different in the future: I'll give up the demon drink,
My behaviour will be lady-like and sober.
But call me back before I change to tell me what you think.
I could start next month – or wait until October.

Do nothing in a hurry was my mother's sound advice,
And, after all, some skittishness is charming.
A triple gin – much later – would be really rather nice,
When I'm merry I am thoroughly disarming.
Your next-best friend, I recollect, laughed loudly at one pun
And said he found staid women somewhat boring.
As I danced and flirted madly, he declared that I was fun.
Better wake him up now. I can hear him snoring.

1

CURTAINS

She's always early, harassing the bell
to let her in before the party starts,
paying all bills the moment they arrive
as though time's passing her in overdrive.
She sits in empty theatres, apart,
waiting for life-lines, running parallel.

He's always late, missing the warm-up scenes.
The minutes pop, quick bubbles, now he's here,
a life evaporating in champagne
and yet time stretches on another plane.
Take care of seconds and the spinning years
will care for him, breathless and evergreen.

They meet half-way in someone else's hall:
she's leaving as he enters but a chime
catches them both as Cupid's arrow strikes –
too late? too early? This midnight is like
a tale told by a pander. He's in time
to turn her round. She waits. Her taxi calls.

ENHANCEMENT

She forms in his real eyes as he downloads
the icon of her smile, her taut, white skin,
it's slow, it always is, it discommodes

his system when he meets her face to face.
There's something not quite right – so he begins
to mouse-click on his clip-art database.

Some small adjustments, tweakings, to her lips,
nose, hairline, shoulder-angle … underpin
her breasts with Sellotaping finger-tips.

The arrow grows, surrenders to desire,
he's finished touching her: she's raked, cool, thin,
his hands will never move beyond the wire:

she's screened the way she wanted it to be
when she first glossed her brows with glycerine
and starved a little more each day. She's free

to satin-out, to lie in air-tight rooms,
licensed to stroke the clean sheet, imagine
that he is coming – not yet – but too soon.

SCRAMBLED

The code-book for his next move lies inside
his left breast pocket, waterproofed. It keeps
the keys and algorithms dry. She weeps
twice nightly but the oilskin's fortified.

It's strong against her tears: she cannot guess
what old words mean, the ones once used to her.
She tests their frequency – 'love' does recur:
when she taps in a question he says 'yes'.

But careless repetition makes a blip,
cryptographers grow lazy, cillies give
a chink for her to crack his narrative.
He's working late again at brinkmanship.

She holds his unwrapped heart in her right hand
and throws it, with its secrets, in the bin.
The tea-leaves write a plaintext bulletin:
he'll read it, smile, try to misunderstand.

PARTNERS

I)

She'd love him if she could but there's no choice:
she can't perceive him even though she tries,
straining to see his face or hear his voice.

What's happened? When she married him her eyes
encountered firm material and weight,
a man her nerves and hands must recognise.

Since then, he's vanished. Diaries can't date
the moment when his nose first slipped away
or hair and toes began to separate.

His outline quavered, wobbled. Day by day
he blurred and melted: red lips, blue-black hair,
brown eyes evaporated into grey.

By habit, she accepts that he's still there –
so nods and reaches out to silent air.

II)

She's there for him but she's a palimpsest,
the manuscript of self is overlaid,
well hidden under layers and seventh best.

She was clear once, on top, her form displayed
in all he saw, her whisper was a shout
startling his lust and never disobeyed.

Then, not quite consciously, he rubbed her out,
starting with just her lips and in their place
dropped bee-stung swellings in a different pout.

Soon he'd sketched in a new, familiar face,
made up from bits of girls he'd known before
and after. Then her body. Watch this space.

It's limitless as long as he can draw
comparisons to make her less – or more.

5

CALCULATORS

By what arithmetic does she compute
his value, his entire, essential sum?
Sex plus keen shoulders, full mouth, loose-cut suit;
do these add up to what he may become?
She edits out his figure, prostitutes
the present for the future. With her thumb
she taps in numerals of fatherhood,
the little keys of 'ought' and 'must' and 'should.'

By what geometry does he outline
her shapes, her points and her mysterious arcs?
Pythagoras can't help him now. "She's mine,"
the proof is there: he joins up all the marks
of love she's made and, like the columbine,
they tangle round his youth. Her thighs, her dark
complexities – he thinks he's drawn them right,
ruling out error: 'could' and 'would' and 'might.'

DECONSTRUCTION

He intertexts his story: 'I,' 'you,' 'she'
fall (harmlessly?) from his slow-writing lips.
I've read him for a year, a refugee
from my own life to his – no censorship,
no barriers to his talk on pillowslips.
This version is my book and all my clues;
'she's' had a different discourse, differing cues
for entrances and exits yet the plot ...
the plot's the same old tale of me and you
and some-one else, black-balled from Camelot.

So, as I listen, little 'ah's' and 'oo's'
encrypt my interest in a microdot
of female filming over: true? untrue?
He'll never know – or put me on the spot,
I am the lucky one; he's my jackpot.
But 'she,' beyond the margin, guarantees
herself a place between us: I can see
her shadow on the sheet, her fingertip
pointing to words he's skewed from her to me:
lust/love – which one? The sword above me dips.

CONTINUUM

All night we lay, divided, back to back,
I sensed the careful curve of your cold spine,
six inches distant)(measured, just like mine:
entrenched, dug-in and ready to attack:
the Xerox of each other's line is drawn.
Outside, the curtained sky slides into dawn.

Morning, in seamless change, will move to noon,
fog becomes mist and winter clears to spring.
I told you not to interrupt the string
of functions in my heart – look how the moon
phases itself, and me. Now I grow full,
my blood-tides running high from push to pull.

I cannot help myself – the tug's too much,
I turn towards you, flowing into reach
and pluck your arm like wave-tips on the beach
with urgent finger-ends. You roll and touch
my shoulder with one hand. Your palm feels rough
but makes a gentle joining. That's enough.

HOW WAS IT FOR YOU?

The praying mantis never asks her mate
this fatal question. Now that you're not there
I also know I've left it rather late
to hear your answers to my questionnaire.
We only did it once. I tried my best,
employing many touches meant to please.
I always thought a woman should suggest
some small refinements – and that slow striptease
was not intended to take quite so long.
My other lovers liked my raunchy style,
my energy, my comments. Was I wrong
to wake you up to go that extra mile?
      And when I nibbled at your sweet right ear,
      why did you shiver? Was it lust, my dear?

ENTROPY

Even at first, your eyes were temperate.
(I loved their grey) so balanced, clear and cool,
you spoke of level planes, derided those
who loved with heat, which then must dissipate.
Covertly one such, I became your fool
and proved you right, as ever. At the close

of our – what shall I say? – relationship
your coldness matched my disillusionment,
no warmth of mine lay ashen in your eye.
I once had read that energy must slip
away and fade, but how and where it went
is still unknown. No matter how I try

to reckon, the equation is the same:
the answer tells me that some love is lost
on each exchange till we arrive at nought.
Pre-warning me, you are absolved from blame;
not heeding you, I paid the total cost –
to find my knowledge is too dearly bought.

MOMENTUM
in an isolated system

Unchanging over time, momentum shifts
from bat to ball and yet is never lost.
I take your hand in mine, a movement swift
as panic and transfer the coin I tossed.

Still as a death, with motion held, we wait,
not even trembling, tied yet separate.

The silver lies between our palms: we know
that energy rests somewhere in this pause.
No-one decides whether to stay or go
as I withdraw my sudden hand from yours.

POINTS

North
sends moss
to tree bark
and resting stones.
Move with me, love, where love can be increased.

West
paints red
on true hearts:
but must love set
and die? Hold me in
twilight and henceforth.

East
throws light
through curtains
where love's awake
with never-weary
eyes, lips, skin and mouth.

South
pours heat
of noon-day,
augments our love
until it encompasses us, possessed.

FLAMSTEED

Precision-minded, he must chart the skies
in icy solitude from his small shed,
plot ancient constellations, analyse
a life-time's observations. Overhead
circles the only company he keeps,
a glittering society, as bright
as courtly gossip. Duty never sleeps:
forty-three years he watches, night by night
roof-shutters back, he measures points in space,
rotating in a stately minuet.
He has his own meridian, his base
of accuracy as stars rise and set.
        They make him publish, but he fears, perhaps
        the work's not perfect yet – and burns his maps.

Wren's Octagon Room in the Royal Observatory could not be used since
its meridian was falsely positioned.

ST. SEBOLT

He kindles fire with icicles. The night
burns elemental contrasts: water/flames;
hot/cold; dark/bright. I read and speculate,
imagining his healing hands create
new pyrotechnics, weary of the same
old miracles, rehearsed, jejune and trite.

Does he feel contradictions glow and fight
within himself: sainthood/a human name;
obscurity/celebrity; choice/fate?
Here is his chance to flaunt and strut – not wait
for slow processions of the blind and lame
to grumble past him in this dim twilight.

DR. JOHNSON

He's lumbered with huge flesh and heavy bones,
bent nearly double, twitching, gulping food.
In other men a flame-like mind disowns
the body's weight and its inquietude.
His reason cannot tell him how to live,
how his light soul could fly above disease:
this monstrous carapace will never give
the spirit time to separate with ease.
He knows the two are different but his frame
is so convulsed with crippling, black-dog fears
that in half-madness they become the same.
The wolf gnaws until selfhood disappears.
          And as his mother dies, he sits and writes:
          he'll pay her passage with his darkest nights.

[Johnson's mother made him read *The Whole Duty of Man* every Sunday.
'On hearing she was dying, he did not speed to her bedside but
plunged into writing *Rasselas*, exculpating himself by earmarking the
proceeds for her funeral.' Roy Porter *Flesh in the Age of Reason*.]

PORTRAIT OF THE DUKE OF WELLINGTON: 1814

The eyes have it. Deep in that oblique stare
he's ordering the field and saying yes.
He nods. Cavalry wheels and muskets smoke.
"I will, my Lord." He plays his masterstroke
then gallops off towards the day's success,
blue-blooded, arrogant and debonair.

The nose is shaped for war: it smells defeat
and caution – when it's time to shake the head.
There have been weeks of marching in grey dust
then waiting for the sudden blood-stained thrust,
the chess-board overturned, the wounds' bright red,
black vultures chortling in the Spanish heat.

Arms folded and a canvas blank as peace
scar-brown, a horse's shoulder behind his.
Leave out uncertainty, deck him in braid
and let him join the coloured cavalcade
of alpha males knowing just how it is
renting their fame from us. We own the lease.

THE BATTLE OF SALAMANCA

Vultures in burning skies: they know it's sealed
before Duke Wellington makes up his mind.
The squaddy feels quick panic in his eyes
as armies circle, pause, try to disguise
their faltering nerve. Now only man is blind;
the birds see harvests ripening in the field.

Behind the lines, Scovell, code-breaker, sweats:
the numbers in the cipher tell of troops
innumerable, as the French regroup.
They prey on him, black figures, silent threats.

Ten days ago, on the Duero's banks,
the soldiers, on both sides, laughed, bowed and waved,
watered their horses in a stream of peace,
washing their hands of death in a release
of hope that some, some few, refreshed and shaved
might live in cleanliness. "Merci!" "Yes, thanks."

An army marches on the strength of codes:
their Paris cipher's weaker than his brain.
He reads the messages en clair again.
That's it: the mini-armistice explodes.

Thunder that night, the battle's autocue:
great horses rear in images of war,
dragoons are trampled but the day breaks clear;
the times have gone for hope or even fear,
those vultures long for redness on the claw.
The General cries: "By God, sir! This will do!"

THE RACE TO PARIS: 1914

The French *poilu*, foot-soldier, packs his kit
with everything he needs to live and kill
the other man. He forms a pyramid:

spare socks in case his boots chafe – and they will!
entrenching tool, field dressing, bayonet,
his rifle, ammunition pouch. He's filled

his *chargement de campagne* and so he sets
the metal cooking pot on top – and smiles:
his dinner is the last thing he'll forget.

His *brodequins* must march for twenty miles
each sky-blue day: he plods on bleeding feet
through heavy August. One warm night he piles

an earthy cassoulet in his *marmite*,
eats mightily, then scrubs it mirror-clean.
His regiment tramps on; the ears of wheat

rise, hide the men, but shafts of sunlight beam,
reflected on the pots. A sniper shoots,
(it's young Lieutenant Rommel) hits the gleam.

They all marched on their stomachs in pursuit
of schedules that would lead them to Verdun.
Some will get there ... while quick success en route

fires up the junior marksman with the gun
as he reflects on victory in the sun.

PREDICTION

A single raindrop hits a mountain ridge,
sharp-edged and high, dividing East from West.
He looks at his computer screen, he's guessed
which way this storm will blow. His foreknowledge
depends upon small, chancy things: a midge
could flap its wings, a heron wag its crest
to kick-start chaos; and the only test
is in the losing-out, the haemorrhage.
If A falls right it will flow on to Z;
he dare not move, his finger's paralysed,
he dare not love – but hearts that miss a beat
can cause a deluge too. The watershed
waits for a little bloodspot, undersized
but spilt for her, messy and incomplete.

LOSING IT

She's learned Newton's hard laws, now she needs π
to find one particle, identify
its present state, then where it goes – and why.

If she could track them all, she would predict
tomorrow, next year, cock a snook at strict
old Matron Nature's rule, now derelict.

But that Greek letter, footling little sign,
escapes her, figures grow along a line
towards the infinite and fool's moonshine.

What can she do? She doesn't know but she
plays with equations, numbers, whilst the free
chaos of clouds swirls round a chestnut tree.

Don't laugh at her. She's doing what she must,
impelled, whip-driven by a wanderlust,
a need for termini, something to trust.

It seemed so simple, back in school, to write
approximations on the board: clear, white
chalked certainties and answers. Now, tonight ...

... she might as well toss coins, call heads or tails,
guess probabilities, skid off the rails;
she puts a 10p piece on her thumbnail.

Flipping, spinning for ever, so it seems,
the silver forms a fish in twilight streams,
blurred body as the edgy backbone gleams.
She's lost, at last: it won't come down; she dreams
of water flowing far beyond her schemes.

The precise value of π is virtually impossible to calculate, though it may
sometimes be needed to invoke chaos theory from the behaviour of
particles and foretell future events.

20

HOW TO DOODLE THE FIBONACCI SEQUENCE

I draw a zero, then think of a rabbit,
Sketch its furred outline in Indian ink,
Ears at the ready lest Reynard should nab it,
I draw a zero – then think.

Rabbits are cool but they breed in disorder,
Six have appeared out of nowhere. I need
Much more control – so I rule a neat border.
Rabbits are cool, but they breed.

Go back to nought and add one. My black figures
Look rather dull after rabbity fun.
Maybe they'll jazz up as they get much bigger:
Go back to nought and add one.

One, two, three, five, eight … I pause and consider:
It's exponential and soon there'll be scores,
All from that first 0, that primagravida,
One, two, three, five, eight. I pause.

Thirteen comes next – but I'm brave and shall press on,
At least these digits know how to behave,
Weaving their spirals in magic progression,
Thirteen comes next, but I'm brave.

Seeds on the sunflower grow like this series,
Complex perfection – and somehow I know
This is the answer to everyone's queries:
Seeds on the sunflower grow.

Leonardo Pisano derived the Fibonacci sequence, in which each term is
the sum of the preceding two numbers, from a recreational problem
involving fertile rabbits in the Liber Abaci, 1202.

OPTICAL

"There is no light or colour as a fact in external nature. There is merely motion of material". Alfred North Whitehead.

Defined by greenness, emeralds cheat
to catch my eyebeam as I pass;
there is no radiance in the grass,
each blade's a spinner of deceit.

I am traduced at every glance
by pigments in soft, cushioned moss,
by particles that double-cross
my nerves and brain in joined-up dance.

Is this, then, the material state:
minutiae in endless fuss,
sans colour, light, except for us;
I realise, thus I create?

Beauty's not Truth: the poor fool,
the poet hazarding a guess,
made an equation out of mess,
an abstract law from dark misrule.

Too young to know, perhaps too green
to think that he must give the kiss
of life, the human genesis,
to things not there until they're seen.

ALLEGRO
ma non troppo

Someone conducts this garden from a score
marked with restraint: 'Be bright but not too much.'
The fuchsia nods consent, the fennel waves
agreement – and they try – but on the staves
of branches hang too many notes. I touch
fruit, petals, leaves and hear the brightness pour.

It's overgrown with colour, quick and light
and far too much to keep within the plot:
the maestro can't control these laden plums;
blackcurrants riot as the quince tree drums
a roll ... they're on a roll ... they're off ... but not
allegro any more – and much too bright.

PUTTING THE CLOCKS FORWARD

Passing from room to room, I change their hands
to mark an hour lost; a small attempt
at synchronising stars to our routines.
My moving fingers play the go-between:
suns wait for me to check them and pre-empt
the waywardness of time with my commands.

Out in the garden on a plinth of stone
the ancient dial shows it can't be done:
shadows will fall as they fell yesterday
and no-one makes the silver birch obey.
Deep underground a summer has begun,
without permission, riotous, unknown.

INTRODUCING THE HOP

The trellis arch wants something to disguise
its creosoted newness. Her plan needs
a careful purchase, one that shoots and spreads
untamed, to contrast with the flowerbeds
so neatly planted, innocent of weeds,
an Eden for the snake to recognise.

Off to the garden centre. Soon the hop
has settled in, surging its lime-green leaves
on serpent stalks, curling into the air,
sticky, persistent, catching in her hair
as she ducks past. It has designs on Eve's
serenity. She knows it. This must stop.

Her armoury lies ready on the shelf:
white cotton gloves, bright sharpened secateurs.
But intertwining stems reach round her waist,
entangling her in wildness, a foretaste
of fallen pleasures that could still be hers
if she would lose the plot and find herself.

SOLIPSISM

A twig falls from the silent silver birch
and clatters on the roof of my old shed;
startled, I pause, give up the cobwebbed search
for half-full seed-packets. The flowerbeds
mist over, fade ... this noise has filled my mind
with rips-raps, fire-crackers and left me blind.

The little, fatal landing amplifies
and I hear bombs, glass breaking and my ears
have stolen all my nerve cells, closed my eyes
in panic as the garden disappears.
I force my hands to reach out to a shelf
and touch warm, dusty wood to earth myself.

Back come the smells, the compost and the lawn,
I taste the sun again and everything
jigsaws into its place; bud, leaf and thorn,
the pattern's finished and a blackbird sings.
I hear a sudden frog's full-throttled croak
and – look – a greenness gathers round the oak.

JUNE 30th

It feels as though the summer's still to come
as heat spreads through the house and weights the air.
Schoolchildren watch thin sunbeams dance with dust
and cities wait for holidays elsewhere;
expectancy beats like a muster drum.

But calendars and diaries deceive:
these thirty days have held an equinox;
Midsummer's Eve has gone and wanderlust
hangs on the cheating of our kitchen clocks.
They sing of golden hours and we believe.

The gardener knows better as he bends
to snip dead roses. His hands sense swift time
passing to seed, his hardened fingers trust
flowers to tell him when they're past their prime
and some are speaking now of distant ends.

PROCRASTINATION

The old shed, in the corner, shadowed now
by sycamores and beech leaves, dark and cool,
waits for the sun to climb above that bough,
beam in through cobwebbed windows, warm the tools'
smoothed handles, ready for my hands. I wait
a little longer for the heavy heat,
leave spades alone until it is too late,
let spiders silk them over. Sacks of peat
spill open, compost dries; the smell of sheds
at noon is like a manacle. I'm trapped
by broken rakes, empty seed-trays. My head
buzzes with sleep-thoughts ... musty ... must ... perhaps ...
      I dream of camomile: no need to mow
      my cruel lawn today – or tomorrow.

DROUGHT

This summer has forgotten how to rain,
my pond turns greener than the sallow grass
and shrinks down in its liner. Goldfish rise
greedy for oxygen; dim, bulbous eyes
of frogs glare at my sandals as I pass.
Nothing can move the brutal weathervane.

Harsh blue has governed since the coup of Spring,
the take-over by April's sudden heat,
flaming and burning earth and careless skin.
Small clouds wave their white flags to underpin
the sun's dictatorship. I hear a bleat
from distant sheep greeting the golden king.

Alone I dream of grey relief and think
of evening showers with their quickening drops,
of falling mercury and low, damp air,
a rainbow saving minnows from despair.
I almost hear intoxicated plops
as toads jump back. Now let the lilies drink!

SEPTEMBER

Uncertain, in this garden, seasons move
marked by the relaxation of a rose
and two leaves falling. Dew invades my feet;
I am the one, the only one, to know
that ice will come to take the tamed foxglove.

But out there, out at sea, the waves have found
new forces, winter power: they crash and swell
on colder shingle, warn me to retreat.
I have no salt moon almanacs to tell
me what they only know or who they've drowned.

I'll walk away from gardens, run from shores,
leave scattered petals, driftwood – except one
still-open flower and useful log. I cheat
the darkening world, defeat the watery sun
with vases, fires, dry thoughts behind thick doors.

SEPTEMBER EQUINOX

A temporary truce when day and night
lay down their hours of equal black and white
      in autumn armistice,
a balance in the skies: darkness and light
are poised in friendliness as if they might
      suspend themselves like this.

But peace is always somewhat hit-and-miss,
there's no eternal hug or endless kiss.
      Too soon the waiting shade,
held for the moment in paralysis,
will make a move. No human artifice
      can make it feint or fade.

Winter must win and march its chill parade
of leafless, figured trees and ponds inlaid
      by frost. But now the sight
of dew not ice on every resting blade
sheathed in the lawn (and midges unafraid)
      postpones the flight-or-fight.

KNITTING

The lawn is mown, its careful edges cut,
trimmed into random curves, casting off greens
from aquilegia, cornflowers. Eyes half-shut,
I half-dream colours, shades of dried has-beens
and sense October's propped-up guillotine.
It will come down, that blade, that winterkill
and sever this from this with sudden chill:
birds, leaves, stalks, midges, petals sequestrate
themselves for months; those intertwined tendrils
of bindweed slacken, die and separate.

Sad? No – just feel it falling with the thrill
of endings, closure and the steady state
where nothing grows or merges, an idyll,
a hopeless island, ice-bound, safe. I wait
for cold, for cloud. Certainty amputates
soft foolishness of summer and the glut
of swollen blackberries, split hazel-nuts.
This moment is dark reason's go-between:
better the devil known, no ifs or buts –
locked doors, control and everything foreseen.

DEAR MR HOUSMAN

This spring I walked, remembering your words,
watching the blossom shadows on the lawn;
then, looking upwards, noticing a bird
amongst etched petals. Perfect. Overdrawn
on time, I left the laden cherry tree
for phone calls, letters, bills and cluttered mess.
I should have stayed, my feet on filigree
of leaf and flower fractals. I confess
I knew its ivy-covered trunk had split
and rotted ... but "It's been like that for years."
(The trick is in the guessing when to quit.)
It's gone now, axed, but I am sitting here
        in autumn sunlight, waiting for the gold
        of fruitwood fires and winter's silvered cold.

PUTTING THE CLOCKS BACK

A cooling sun shrinks slowly down the sky
as goldfish sink in black depths of the pond,
sap slides to roots, a vortex of dry leaves
whirls for a moment. Nothing here deceives
the human onlooker who sees beyond
bright scarlet rose-hips, this last butterfly.

Winter will come, dark fingers write plaintext
on trees and shrubs; we read these ancient signs:
this one means frost, that signifies a storm,
grey months when only circling blood is warm.
October days are pointers on a line
way-marked with arrows, next leads on to next.

Why wait? Why tremble? Let the chill winds blow:
we'll move the night, let it arrive an hour
before its time. We will not live with doubt,
we'll tinker till we nudge the summer out.
Here is our certainty, now clocks empower
our hands and fingers to bring on the snow.

WATCH IT

It sounds like repetition – but the same
small noise, a tick or tock, changes its tune:
the air is different, the note disclaims
that this time measures a flat afternoon.
The little hills and downsides of each hour,
minute or nanosecond, shift the hands
and half-past twelve is poles apart as our
memory of yesterday no longer stands.
The ditto marks of past years cheat and lead
us to find patterns, replications, yet
the signs are changing, falsely – we misread
old runes and make an ordered alphabet.
      The comfort of clock fingers on the dot
      gives us a narrative, a counterplot.

FAMILY PLANNING

Twelve months before a birth, the baby waits,
choosing its parents (putative) with care.
It fancies Simon's nose and Sarah's hair
but they're not even flirting. It would hate
Robert's slipped chin and mottled ears or Kate's
sour tendency to acne. Unaware,
two party-goers magnetise and pair.
There is a future world to populate.
As Joe and Stephanie meet, chat and kiss
our insubstantial Cupid shoots his darts,
the little laughing boy hits home. He means
to tranquillise them long enough for this:
their perfect wedding of true minds and hearts;
his pick-and-mix selection of sweet genes.

IT'S A ...

Darkly, unknown, her double-helix rips,
one half swaps places, joins itself to his,
a new encoding as the spiral zips.

They don't know what they've done, the messages
in secret letters spell out hair and nose,
dictate each toenail, write it as it is.

The blob of cells, still splitting, grows and grows
in silent transmutation to an end
half-feared, hidden, determined days ago.

An interlacing chain, a random blend
of his and hers, a mongrel magi-mix
of chemicals, a game of break-and-mend.

They're wondering what it's like as the clock ticks:
the answer's in Pandora's box of tricks.

CONCEPTION

Her fair hair waits, a rival to his brown
and, as he kisses her, their lips compete.
Soon, on this night, her footprints will bear down

and his will lose the race. Now their eyes meet,
blue upon blue; legs, hands, the shape of bones
fight for a placing, as their codes repeat

dark, ancient messages, unseen, unknown.
A chain forms from the past; their baby son
will link them evermore. They can't disown

this clew to history, this thread they've spun.
Tomorrow they will talk and hope as she
hugs to herself a marriage just begun,

a knot of cells tied to them by decree,
struggling to grow, to break away and be.

THE ORIGIN OF SPECIES

A little random flick of DNA,
a chance mutation, taking hold, admits
that slight advantage – and a species splits.
The faster big cat hurtles on its way
towards the juiciest, slow-moving prey.
The fittest will survive, the one that fits
its niche the best, fights on and never quits
or takes a careless, lounging holiday.
I know that's how it is, and was, but I
wonder sometimes about that jewelled watch,
that fish's eye, this new black jaguar's paw,
the flashing mystery of a damselfly.
I turn the winder backwards, notch by notch
and find a clock-maker – above the law.

GOD FORMULATES A LONG-TERM STRATEGIC PROJECT

By the sixth lunch-break, most of it was done:
light, water, chaos sorted, new dry land,
moon, stars and (top banana) a huge sun,
fish, animals, all just as He had planned.
But now He thinks this Earth-job might be manned
so that He could appear as God of Love,
a type of Father figure up above.

Rhinoceroses, bless them, have no soul
and who has seen a crayfish lost in prayer?
His mission statement must include a goal
without descending to the doctrinaire:
'They'll worship Me from Prague to Aberdare.'
He'll program humans destined to believe –
but there's a software glitch in making Eve.

A kind of virus or invading worm
must have been lurking in young Adam's rib
and maybe, Heaven help us, in his sperm:
a tendency (genetic) to ad-lib,
then cover up with fig leaves and a fib.
And if He gives these bastards long enough,
they'll cast Him off and strut their worldly stuff.

He needs eye-catching visions for the next
millennia, at least, but His brain numbs.
Now Adam goes astray (too over-sexed,
one bite from that first Cox and he succumbs
to the eternal lure of tits and bums.)
Tomorrow's Sunday, dress-down time – He'll hide,
consider all His options and decide.

DEVOLUTION

Day Six, late morning, He makes a baboon,
looks at it shrewdly, notes its main defect.
That bottom! Never mind – this afternoon
He'll do a hairless one that walks erect,
a human He can train to genuflect:
two or three tweakings to the basic shape
and a small brain-box. Lo! a thinking ape.

Tight-arsed and clever, Man leaves Paradise,
holding her hand and, damn it, set to breed
(they lack the spirit of self-sacrifice.)
Now Reason, like a new, pernicious weed,
spreads through their minds and starts to cast its seed.
God spends His Sunday with the crystal ball
of His omniscience – and dreads it all.

He sees a long line (starting with the Greeks)
of nuisances, versed in philosophy.
Minds honed by Jesuitical techniques
and prating on about ontology,
they raise objective questions vis-à-vis
His own existence till they rub Him out
and crucify Him with their nails of doubt.

Yet when they're harmless they are still a feature
that He would not, by choice, have factored in.
Who in their proper mind would dream up Nietzsche
or even part-believer Augustine,
two Humes (one 'l'), Spinoza and Darwin,
the greatest trouble-maker of the lot.
God sighs and plans a craft counterplot.

With secret cunning He'll divide and rule
to render them innocuous and bland.
He nudges some of them towards a school
of language analysts, a probing band
(Vienna-based) who aim to understand
only the words that they themselves must use,
internal logic, decked with curlicues.

ON THE EIGHTH DAY

In retrospect the work had been great fun.
He'd always thought Himself a technophobe
but He'd made, on His own, a mighty sun,
a world of things from mountain to microbe.
Today, He thinks, He'll build another one,
a kind of toy, a palm-held mini-globe,
but perfect in its way, scaled, spick and span,
with all the big Earth had, except for Man.

Nothing this time will bugger up His scheme.
He finds some magma, pops on bits of crust,
a pimple for an Alp, a thread-like stream
for little crocodiles. He sprinkles dust
in coffeespoons for deserts. Now His dream
is coming to fruition and He must
switch on the light. The revolutions start
and one volcano puffs a tiny fart.

He looks at it that night and finds it good,
so *ecological*: no nasty mess
of greenhouse gases; hacking down of wood
needed next year. The hour has come to bless
this new creation and He knows He should.
How Jupiter will envy His success!
(He's glad he told that couple they must leave.
Ah – there goes Adam hand in hand with Eve.)

SPARKIE

He's come to wire the house. With second-sight
he looks through ceilings, floorboards: here he might
    thread coils and over there
hang a quick lamp, a glowing stalactite.
Ideas take root, spread out and soon his sleight
    of hand moves everywhere.

Prometheus in overalls. His flair
presumes against the darkness, he will dare
    to torch these rooms and fill
my little world with *son et lumière*,
He's mastermind, producer and compère
    of his great vaudeville.

My life is now the focus of his skill,
the hidden pantomime, silent until
    he calls for opening night.
I am my only audience. I will
applaud the switching-on, sitting quite still;
    he speaks: "Let there be light."

"THE POSSIBILITY OF ANGELS"
(Derek Walcott)

Perhaps the wind has wiped away their prints,
their heel-marks from the sand – and in the air
above the coast of St. Lucia, hints
of feathered spaces flicker here, there, there.

Gulls or white sanderlings could trick an eye
too willing to believe. That emptiness
within the heart, transferred to earth or sky
demands a seraph, sends an S.O.S.

An island is an Eden but the snake
wriggles inside a green, aspiring mind:
a little hiss of worlds elsewhere can make
or break you: "Leave that paradise behind!"

You too have feet to stay and wings to go,
apples to eat. As you stand on the cliff,
look seawards, angel; only men are slow
at taking off, weighted by 'but' and 'if'.

HER UNCONSCIONABLE LIGHTNESS

Just like the specks floating across his eyes,
she shimmies past a backdrop of grey air.
He cannot help but watch her. Now he tries
to shut his lids, blank out, yet still she's there
within his veins, freewheeling everywhere.
She is his trivial girl in gauzy blue,
fabrics by Ghost, her shoulders gleaming through,
pale lipstick, thin, head in a magazine
or pressed against her mobile. Honeydew
drips from her mouth, not words. She's seventeen.

He'd like to ground her, weight her strappy shoes,
fill her with thoughts, become a go-between,
link her to this real world, transmit his views.
He'll be her ballast, he will intervene,
leave nothing dancing, nothing unforeseen.
First catch the prey. His insubstantial prize
slips from his speech-trap, suddenly too wise
to walk the earth. One foot is near the snare:
babies are waiting and the newborn cries.
She flicks her wings, tosses her drifting hair.

THAT DRESS

A snake-skin print, silk-lined and ankle length;
it shimmers on the hanger out of reach
of her right hand and purse. Bright blood runs hot
along her left arm in a counterplot.
Three credit cards are burning and with each
she could set fire to Ilium's ancient strength.

She'd launch a thousand ships in viscose, cut
close to her moulded shoulders, serpent hips.
Inside the changing room, she hears the beat
of hearts and drums as minds are in retreat.
She angles in the mirror; yet her lips
part for a moment, breathe one cool word: 'but'.

Someone will pay for this great surge of lust,
this rush of heat, this trembling to possess.
She can't afford to sign, but she's for sale.
Will armies fight for her? Her face is pale
as she slips out with that too-costly dress.
Someone will pay, not her, but someone must.

FIRST TIME

One suitcase – finite. Her thin bed is strewn
with shorts, strap-sandals, wrapped transparent soap
and lotions to transform her Monday skin.
Things, irreducible, to underpin
a fortnight somewhere else with packaged hope
of touching Dionysus and Neptune.

She needs another bag; then off she flies
burdened with too much forethought. Wine and sea
are waiting, frothing, tumbling as her blood
speeds up, impelled by thoughts half-understood.
The hairy, restless gods reach out and she
quickens, unpacks herself, loosens her thighs.

Nothing could make her ready for the salt
of foreign air, her first deep, gasping breath:
rank with desire, like olives in the sun,
falling into strong waves that run and run
until she's finished and a sudden death
returns her to that thin bed – by default.

WAKE-UP CALL

Last night they didn't. Why does she feel used,
flinching from him in bed? Her untouched skin
wants to protect itself, its layers so thin
than even thoughts of sex can leave her bruised.
His back is turned in sleep. She lies accused
of his indifference; she cannot win
this stand-off or recall its origin,
the moment when he begged to be excused.
His absent hands are clenched as if to hit:
wham, pow, and she curls up making to hide.
Foetus or woman? Sheets become a womb
for a few moments and then, bit by bit,
something returns, the devil-prick of pride:
it's not an everywhere, this little room.

SLEEPING

Beneath our floorboards, biros, paperclips,
a picnic spoon, still dirty, lie in wait.
A rabble of lost plastic sulks: one day
they'll get together, rise and infiltrate
our ordered rooms, our neat relationships.

And so will little words we've dropped, the blips
in half-forgotten discourses: 'I hate …'
'you are too …' 'never', now in disarray,
could plan an ambush, charge and liberate
your head and mine from laundered pillowslips.

TAKE YOUR PICK

Of the two different types of sloth,
the three-toed is more moribund,
lethargic, comatose, though both
look lackadaisical, half-stunned.

It naps three-quarters of the day,
hangs out above the forest floor,
no creature covets it as prey:
its hygiene is so very poor

that parasites thrive in its hair.
It sleeps alone but once a week
it feels a bit more debonair,
climbs slowly down to take a peek

at local social life – perhaps
that's when it hopes to find a mate,
compete with all the other chaps
who dawdle, loaf, snooze, vegetate

till Saturday, at half past two,
then kick off, dirty, self-obsessed,
malodorous, assuming you
and I are easily impressed.

We're not: we are distinctly loath
to listen to his lazy voice
but, like the three-toed female sloth –
it seems we haven't got much choice.

THE POET DECIDES TO SPRING CLEAN

Too many words: the wardrobes of his soul,
(heart, psyche, brain) are packed with synonyms,
so full that he can't find the right *bon mot*.
Old similes, thought up a year ago,
clutter his mind, mothballed, seeming to him
to interbreed in dusty cubby-holes.

They separate and mix like ancient socks,
as dull as cucumbers, no longer cool.
What can he do with fraying metaphors,
worn at the seams and fading out in drawers?
Limp adjectives hang in the vestibule;
he takes one down, reveals a paradox.

He needs the muddle to spin magic lines
and yet he's lost in excess. If he throws
this phrase away he might miss it next week.
His mystery lies in playing hide-and-seek:
from that dark, squirrelled mess a poem grows.
Look, in the corner, where a sentence shines.

REGARDING THE CRYSTAL

I hold it by its poles between my thumb
and index finger pad against the light,
a simple transformation: it's become

the prism for a poem. Can I write
something hard, flashy, sharp-edged, permanent,
formed out of essence, layering bright on bright?

This notion, like a sun-shaft, can be bent
by my glass mind to scatter rainbows, arcs,
refracted till you wonder what I meant.

What does a crystal mean? A trick of quarks?
An ambiguity of protons shot
as waves and particles? My inky marks

ripple, bombard, fire colours. Tiny dots
aimed at the 'i's' change everything and puns
form spectra from what is and what is not.

"She'll have no truck with metaphor ..."
[Jacqueline Brown: Thinking Egg]

but I dig them, particularly mixed,
love them to bits then patch them up again.
The literal's too rational, too fixed,
too straight for someone of my acumen.
Yet I'll not be a pig in any manger
sulking because of too-high sour grapes;
I'll walk the plank of truth, though fiction's stranger
and keep the mirror of my mind ship-shape.
My cup is running over, food for thought,
I never look a gift-horse in the stable
and my old gran sucks eggs but can't be taught
new tricks or make an omelette. I am able
        to nip more rats in bud than I can say:
        I'm hoist by my own trumpet every day.

THE PET GOLDFISH TO THE LADY POET
[a response to Wendy Cope's "Being Boring"]

If you call yourself boring, give one thought to me;
My days are spent circling and gazing.
Vicarious thrills are my sole guarantee
Of excitement. I am paraphrasing
When I mention with glee your tempestuous past
(Please forgive me if there's some misquoting)
But I loved the turmoil, I wished it would last,
I adored the excessive emoting.

Head down on your desk you shed oceans of tears,
I watched your tumultuous weeping,
Aware of your hangovers, neurotic fears,
Angst, complexes, problems with sleeping.
Then I had the best of the old Chinese curse:
Schadenfreude and rather smug gloating
Filled my times with interest. Things are much worse
Now that you have eschewed all emoting.

But I'm philosophic, I think as I swim
Alone in a clear world of water.
I'd like to destroy your liaison with him.
I'd like to, but I didn't oughter.
I'll fake a strange sickness since life's so humdrum:
Dull eyes, a weird manner of floating
(Perhaps upside down?) – yes, that way I'll become
Epicentral to your fresh emoting.

"May you live in interesting times" Chinese curse

55

ALTERNATING ROLES

Last week honest Iago; now the Moor
blacks out his mind to all the Ancient's arts:
male bonding, soldiers' trust and soon he's sure
that women, like his wife, are whores and tarts,
each acting, in her time, too many parts.
Yet when he was the villain, he could see
a marriage locked with love. He found the key,
took sex out of the safe, man-handled it,
made himself mad, deaf, blind with jealousy,
playing the biter and the one he bit.

AT HOME

After the curtain's scraped across the stage
closing the final act, the bodies rise,
unscripted, smiling, start to disengage.

Lead 'normal' lives again without disguise?
The motley's off, the stone-washed Levis on:
silence in rooms as echoed clapping dies.

No spotlight when the audience has gone:
Ophelia could drown in tears and weeds
of madness, Lear scream and Oberon ...

without the magic we all vanish, bleed
invisibly, unpainted. Call a friend?
A priest? The doctor? Someone to lip-read.

Someone to tell us what we're saying, end
the shadow-drama. Till then we'll pretend.

THE SURVEYOR IN BED

She's waiting for him, nude. His eyes rehearse
her contours, gentle planes: east/west; north/south
and now they angle down on her, traverse
feet, legs, hips, waist, set markers on her mouth
and breasts. She's lying, ready, on the grid
of his desires and he knows her terrain
by heart and hand: soft, summery, languid;
he has triangulated his domain.
The little copses of dark, curling hair,
meadows of skin and rivers underground
are his and only his – and yet, somewhere,
he hears a jealous Pan-pipe out of bounds.
        A smile plays on her lips: she reaches out
        to touch him with unmeasured notes of doubt.

A MATHEMATICIAN MAKES LOVE

As she lies naked, stretching out her arms,
he estimates the risks, works out their sum.
But love, bright zero, adds on to her charms
tenfold from that one figure. He'll become
an ordinary man, enslaved yet freed:
he cannot think whilst his heart throbs and beats.
From all the complex algebra of need,
will there be answers hidden in these sheets?
Oh yes! The clarifying power of sex
shows him a truth: only the process counts.
He's found the value of mysterious 'x'
and why – in finite, dry-as-dust amounts:
      the proof in mathematics ends with this.
      She turns to him, divides him with a kiss.

CARTOGRAPHER

A globe floats in his mind, a blue balloon
with collage shapes of land and snowy caps.
He pats it with a thought, it drifts away
beyond the prick of pens. He smiles – perhaps
he'll draw it like a dream of ancient maps:
winds with puffed cheeks, sea-monsters, bare-faced moon.

The ink and paint project his world and chart
his hurricanes, deep fears and rising tides,
white soaring peaks and hidden feet of clay.
No-one is lost and nothing falsified.
It's his life-plan and – traveller – your guide,
a flattened, sketchy atlas of the heart.

CARTOGRAPHER'S FOLLY

He pens a perfect map – but is it his,
this transcript of a landscape, mountains, fields
and cliff-top walkway shadowing the shore?
It's nearly finished … one more line … he draws
a small imaginary pond, concealed
within a master-plan of how it is.

If someone copies his life's diagram,
his bleak triangulations, muddy hours,
he's set a trap beneath a real hedge
and he will catch the poacher near the edge
of ownership. Whose is this land? Yours? Ours?
The wolf thinks it's entitled to the lamb.

His little scrap of water, his blue lie,
names him by deed as having squatter's rights
over each knoll, lake, foothill, contour, cirque –
and that's enough. He smiles, rolls up his work,
then goes outside and looks up at the night
tracing a star-bear on the Northern sky.

THE CARTOGRAPHER SLEEPS

He dreams:

This afternoon he steals an hour and naps.
Behind closed lids his eyes scan to and fro,
their rapid movements sketch a world of maps.

The Earth's already finished but below
are strata: sandstone, undivided shale,
all in their coloured shapes. Now he can go

under deep sea roads – he's a diving whale,
measures his length along the ocean floors,
up mountains, down crevasses. Next he'll sail

into the troposphere – he soars and draws
(naming them all) a congeries of clouds:
Bob Cumulus, Jane Cirrus, then explores

even the atoms – christening a crowd
of particles, a gang of isotopes.
He reads his endless register aloud.

All done! A charted universe! His hope?
To sleep again to check for any gaps
caused by God shaking his kaleidoscope.

He has a nightmare:

Cat-napping now, his careful eyeballs trace
firm outlines of once-moving lands, now still
and resting neatly in their proper place.

They have been drawn there by his masterskill,
he's hypnotised these huge   tectonic   plates
but they are only slumbering.
                              They will

wake up   push off   and carelessly create
new structures, unknown continents.   They'll drift
together, mocking as they tessellate.

Or, jokers in his pack of maps,
                              they'll shift
apart   and take with them the bits of names
he's given them: Af   Ind   and every rift

destroys his w o r l d   and all his earthy aims.
The little coloured pieces swell and RAISE
such mountains! He can't measure them or claim

to own those bastard hills as chaos plays
its game of fast and loose. His pillowcase
holds seas of grief and earthquakes of malaise.

OTHER BOOKS FROM SHOESTRING PRESS

HALF WAY TO MADRID: POEMS Nadine Brummer *Poetry Book Society Recommendation*. ISBN 1 899549 70 6   £7.50

BROXTOWE BOY: A MEMOIR Derrick Buttress. ISBN 1 899549 98 6   £8.95

TESTIMONIES: NEW AND SELECTED POEMS Philip Callow. With Introduction by Stanley Middleton. A generous selection which brings together work from all periods of the career of this acclaimed novelist, poet and biographer. ISBN 1 899549 44 7   £8.95

Shoestring Press also publish Philip Callow's novel, BLACK RAINBOW. ISBN 1 899549 33 1   £6.99

TARO FAIR Ian Caws. ISBN 1 899549 80 3   £7.50

THE WEIGHT OF COWS Mandy Coe. ISBN 1 899549 97 8   £7.95

INSIDE OUTSIDE: NEW AND SELECTED POEMS Barry Cole. "A fine poet ... the real thing." *Stand*. ISBN 1 899549 11 0   £6.95

GHOSTS ARE PEOPLE TOO Barry Cole. ISBN 1 899549 93 5   £6.00

SELECTED POEMS Tassos Denegris. Translated into English by Philip Ramp. A generous selection of the work of a Greek poet with an international reputation. ISBN 1 899549 45 9   £6.95

WHO Alan Dent ISBN 1 904886 07 8   £8.95

THE NEW GIRLS Sue Dymoke. ISBN 1 904886 00 0   £7.95

COLLECTED POEMS Ian Fletcher. With Introduction by Peter Porter. Fletcher's work is that of "a virtuoso", as Porter remarks, a poet in love with "the voluptuousness of language" who is also a master technician. ISBN 1 899549 22 6   £8.95

LAUGHTER FROM THE HIVE Kate Foley. ISBN 1 904886 01 9   £7.95

THE HOME KEY John Greening. ISBN 1 899549 92 7   £8.95

LONG SHADOWS: POEMS 1937–2002 JC Hall. ISBN 1 899549 26 9   £8.95

A PLACE APART Stuart Henson. ISBN 1 899549 95 1   £7.95

CRAEFT: POEMS FROM THE ANGLO-SAXON Translated and with Introduction and notes by Graham Holderness. *Poetry Book Society Recommendation*. ISBN 1 899549 67 6   £7.50

ODES Andreas Kalvos. Translated into English by George Dandoulakis. The first English version of the work of a poet who is in some respects the equal of his contemporary, Greece's national poet, Solomos. ISBN 1 899549 21 8   £9.95

OMM SETY John Greening. ISBN 1 899549 51 X £5.95

FIRST DOG Nikos Kavvadias. Translated into English by Simon Darragh
ISBN 1 899549 73 0 £7.95

A COLD SPELL Angela Leighton.*Other Poetry*. ISBN 1 899549 40 4 £6.95

PAGING DOCTOR JAZZ: A Verse Anthology, compiled by John Lucas,
ISBN 1 904886 08 6 £10.00

ELSEWHERE Michael Murphy. ISBN 1 899549 87 0 £7.95

TOUCHING DOWN IN UTOPIA: POEMS Hubert Moore
ISBN 1 899549 68 4 £6.95 Second Printing

MORRIS PAPERS: POEMS Arnold Rattenbury. Includes 5 colour illustrations of
Morris's wallpaper designs. *Poetry Nation Review*. ISBN 1 899549 03 X £4.95

MR DICK'S KITE Arnold Rattenbury, ISBN 1 904886 13 2 £10.00

MAKING SENSE Nigel Pickard. ISBN 1 899549 94 3 £6.00

THE ISLANDERS: POEMS Andrew Sant. ISBN 1 899549 72 2 £7.50

BEHIND THE LINES Vernon Scannell, ISBN 1 904886 02 7 £8.95

MEDAL FOR MALAYA: a novel David Tipton. ISBN 1899549 75 7 £7.95

PARADISE OF EXILES: a novel David Tipton. ISBN 1899549 34 X £6.99

STONELAND HARVEST: NEW AND SELECTED POEMS Dimitris Tsaloumas. This
generous selection brings together poems from all periods of Tsaloumas's life and
makes available for the first time to a UK readership the work of this major
Greek-Australian poet.
ISBN 1 8995549 35 8 £8.00

AT THE EDGE OF LIGHT Lynne Wycherley. ISBN 1 899549 89 7 £7.95

COLLECTED POEMS Spyros L. Vrettos. ISBN 1 899549 46 3 £8.00

TAKE FIVE 04: poems by Shanta Acharya, Clare Crossman, John Gohorry,
Christopher Pilling, Sir John Weston. ISBN 1 904886 09 4 £10.00

For full catalogue write to:
Shoestring Press
19 Devonshire Avenue
Beeston, Nottingham, NG9 1BS UK
or visit us on www.shoestringpress.co.uk